Earth Debates

How Effective Is Recycling?

Catherine Chambers

heinemann
raintree

Edited by Helen Cox Cannons and Jill Kalz
Designed by Steve Mead
Original illustrations © Capstone Global Library Limited 2015
Illustrated by HL Studios, Witney, Oxon
Picture research by Tracy Cummins
Production by Helen McCreath
Originated by Capstone Global Library Limited
Printed and bound in China by CTPS

18 17 16 15 14
10 9 8 7 6 5 4 3 2 1

Library of Congress Cataloging-in-Publication Data
Chambers, Catherine, 1954-
  How effective is recycling? / Catherine Chambers.
     pages cm.—(Earth debates)
Includes bibliographical references and index.
ISBN 978-1-4846-0996-5 (hb)—ISBN 978-1-4846-1001-5 (pb)—ISBN 978-1-4846-1011-4 (eb) 1. Recycling (Waste, etc.)—Evaluation—Juvenile literature. 2. Refuse and refuse disposal—Juvenile literature. I. Title.
  TD792.C53 2015
  363.72'82—dc23   2014013636

This book has been officially leveled by using the F&P Text Level Gradient™ Leveling System.

Acknowledgments
We would like to thank the following for permission to reproduce photographs: Alamy: © imageBROKER, 36, © joeysworld.com, 31, © John Green, 29, © martin berry, 20, © Radharc Images, 35; Aurora Robson: Marshall Coles, 14; Corbis: © Roger Ressmeyer, 7, © Tim Pannell, 41; Getty Images: JEFF J MITCHELL/AFP, 25, Jim Xu, 19, MUNIR UZ ZAMAN/AFP, 37, Oli Scarff, 22, Paula Bronstein, 6, TIMOTHY A. CLARY/AFP, 9; Guadua Bamboo: www.guaduabamboo.com, 24; Newscom: Liang Xu/Xinhua/Photoshot, 18, Niu Shupei/EPN, 23; Purdue Agricultural Communication photo: Tom Campbell, 28; Shutterstock: Atelier A, 26, bogdan ionescu, 32 (plastic), Charles Harker, 8, Huguette Roe, 33, igor.stevanovic, 32 (glass), kao, 32 (metal), KN, 15, leonello calvetti, Cover Middle, Lightspring, 34, Maryna Kulchytska, 32 (wood), Nicram Sabod, 4, Oliver Sved, 16, Roman Samokhin, 32 (paper), stoonn, 17; SuperStock: Ambient Images Inc., 11, Biosphoto, 10, Gardenpix, 21, 27, Universal Images Group, 13; TITECH, 38; Wikimedia: Ignácio Costa, 39.

We would like to thank Professor Daniel Block for his invaluable help in the preparation of this book.

Contents

Some words are shown in bold, **like this**. You can find out what they mean by looking in the glossary.

Why Do We Recycle and What Do We Recycle?

Do you notice how much waste collects in your home and at school? Do you throw things away, then wonder what happens to them? Every year, around the globe, we dump a massive 2.1 billion tons of waste. In the United States alone, the amount of waste thrown away averages out to 4.3 pounds (2 kilograms) per person every day! Surely, it must be better to recycle it? But is recycling actually effective?

❯❯ Plastics, sharp objects, and **toxic** waste litter shorelines all over the world. Volunteers often organize beach-cleaning days throughout the year.

We now know that humans have been recycling things since prehistoric times, when they created new tools from old ones. Recycling waste saves materials and energy. It can be profitable, too. Two hundred years ago, during the Industrial Revolution, businesses sprung up to sell recycled metals and paper. In 1913, an early recycling trade association led to the formation of the Institute of Scrap Recycling Industries (ISRI) in the United States. The ISRI now has 1,600 members and 6,000 facilities in the United States and 30 other countries. Clearly, a lot of people believe that recycling is worth it!

What's involved in recycling?

Waste recycling involves collecting, transporting, sorting, processing, and then reusing a wide range of waste products. These include gases, liquids, solids, and even some invisible atomic waste from power plants. Some waste contains **hazardous** substances, which are harmful to us and the planet, and not all of these can be recycled. So, already we know that recycling all waste is not a possibility. But is it still worth it?

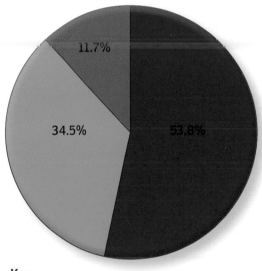

Key:

■ waste in landfills

■ waste recycled or made into compost

■ waste burned for energy

⌃ This pie chart shows that in 2011, over half of the United States' waste ended up in landfill sites.

> **'Solid wastes' are the discarded leftovers of our advanced consumer society. This growing mountain of garbage and trash represents ...a serious economic and public health problem.**
>
> Jimmy Carter, president of the United States from 1977–1981

What happens if we don't recycle?

Some waste materials are **biodegradable**, which means they quickly break down into tiny pieces. These pieces can be **composted** and reused in agriculture or energy production with no harm to people or the planet. However, other materials will be with us for hundreds of years, littering our landscape or piling up in **landfill sites**. Some are toxic, which means they pollute the air, land, and **groundwater**.

Eyewitness

"It's evening time on the Anlong Pi landfill site in Cambodia. Children are scouring the waste to find anything that can be recycled and sold. Here on the site, rainwater acts with harmful chemicals to pollute the soil and groundwater. The air is filled with stifling fumes from burning rubbish."
Using Omar Havana's report for *Al Jazeera*, October 2013

When waste materials are dumped into landfill sites, they break down and produce methane gas. Scientists believe that methane harms our atmosphere, causing global warming. When waste is burned, another harmful gas is **emitted**. This gas is carbon dioxide. Both methane and carbon dioxide are called greenhouse gases, and a blanket of these gases in our atmosphere traps heat on Earth and warms the world's climate.

Workers on landfill sites and dumps can suffer, too. In developing countries, waste pickers go through dumps looking for metal and other items of value. These workers, many of them children, breathe in gases and smoke as they pick waste for recycling.

BIOGRAPHY

David Ross Brower (1912–2000)
David Ross Brower was one of the founders of Friends of the Earth, which works to protect the environment. In 1973, he gave a lecture to support the Village Green Recycling Team, one of New York's earliest community recycling ventures.

California's David Brower Center for the Environment was named in his honor and was built using 53 percent recycled materials.

Do we have too much stuff?

Waste comes from all the goods we produce, buy, consume, and then throw away. But who makes the most waste? One of the largest organizations to collect a lot of data on waste disposal is the World Bank. It has calculated that every year, the richest nations put 276 million tons of waste in landfill sites, while the poorest only throw away 2.4 million tons. The richest nations burn about 134 million tons, while the poorest burn only 55,000 tons. So, do many people in rich countries have too much stuff? Or do they just need to recycle more? Waste collected in richer nations often ends up in landfill sites in poorer nations, for them to sort and recycle.

Did you know?

In 2013, a report listing the seven countries doing the most recycling put Switzerland at the top, with 52 percent of its waste recycled. The next five countries were also from northern Europe. The United States came in seventh, with 31.5 percent. The amount of waste the world produces is increasing by about 3 percent every year.

∧ Landfill sites can be transformed into nature reserves, like this one. But this doesn't always happen.

HERO OR VILLAIN?

Can we trust recycling statistics? The World Bank admits that it is very hard to collect information about waste. Some countries do not count their recycled or composted kitchen waste in their waste total. So, it looks as if these countries only burn their waste or use landfill sites, which is not fair to them. However, it does appear that rich nations are responsible for a lot of full landfill sites and burned waste.

Is Plastics Recycling Effective?

Take a look around you. How many plastic products do you see at home or in school? Take a quick count of all the plastic items in just one small space. Have you ever thought about where they go when you no longer want them?

66 **Without them [plastics], much of modern medicine would be impossible and the consumer electronics and computer industries would disappear. Plastic sewage and water pipes alone have made an immeasurable contribution to public health worldwide.** 99

Norman C. Billingham, professor of chemistry and plastics expert

∨ The sea turtle is one of many marine creatures that mistake plastic bags for food.

Why should we recycle plastics? Well, plastic waste can last for hundreds of years, because most plastics do not break down easily or dissolve. Plastic pollutes every type of environment and habitat, from oceans to deserts. In oceans, discarded plastic bags strangle and choke marine life. After many years in the sea, small pieces of plastic break down into microscopic particles that sea creatures can swallow. On land, plastics are found in groundwater and in the food chain, which means that we swallow them, too!

« Here, scientists are testing water to see if plastics have leached into it, affecting the food chain. As plastics break down, they attract other harmful toxins, too.

HERO OR VILLAIN?

What would life be like without plastics? These amazing materials can be molded into many shapes and easily cleaned. In agriculture, plastic covering retains moisture and warmth in the soil, helping plants to grow in dry or cold places. And in medicine, they are made into lifesaving heart valves, tiny tubes that unblock blood vessels, movable body parts, and much, much more. In the United States alone, the plastics industry employs about 885,000 people.

How do we recycle plastics?

Take a look in your school bag and divide all the plastic items into different types. Simple ballpoint pens, for example, have a hard plastic case, but the inner ink tube is less rigid. You might have an even softer pencil case to put them in. So, you already have three types of plastic. But there are many more, and each needs different treatment for successful recycling.

Plastic types that can be recycled can also easily be reused. Let's take the example of plastic bottles, which are made from recyclable **polymers**. First, they are sorted by the exact type of polymer and by their color. Some are then melted down and reshaped. Others have to be flaked into small pieces before being melted. Recycled bottles are then turned into many different products, such as yard furniture, fleece clothes, and yet more bottles! It takes only 25 two-liter bottles to make one large fleece jacket.

Did you know?

In the United States, in 2012, people generated 32 million tons of plastic. About 14 million tons of this were containers and packaging, about 11 million tons were goods that last such as appliances, and about 7 million tons were disposable goods such as plates and cups. Only 9 percent of this plastic was recovered for recycling. About 25 billion polystyrene foam cups are also discarded annually in the United States.

However, some of the worst effects on the environment come from plastics that cannot be recycled. These include soft plastics, nylon, acrylics, and polystyrene foam used for hot-drink cups and frozen-dinner trays. One of the biggest problems with these plastics is the toxic chemicals used in making them, such as lead, tributyltin, and phthalates, which seep into the soil and groundwater. So, do we need to find ways to recycle these plastics? Or would it be better to find alternative materials?

In Australia, plastic goods are marked with these recycling symbols. South Australia's Zero Waste SA campaign makes a big effort to explain the symbols. Between 2011 and 2012, nearly 80 percent of all waste avoided landfill in South Australia.

Can Hazardous Waste Be Recycled Effectively?

We have seen that plastics contain harmful chemicals, especially when they are burned. But there are even more hazardous forms of waste that need to be disposed of. Is recycling the best way for this?

Do you think there is hazardous waste in your home? Hazardous waste includes cleaning products, paints, **solvents**, fluorescent bulbs, refrigerators, batteries, and **pesticides**. Most homes have a lot of these.

BIOGRAPHY

Aurora Robson (born 1972)
Aurora Robson is a Canadian-born artist who uses waste materials, much of it hazardous, to create large, modern pieces of art. She sometimes uses over 20,000 plastic bottles in creating just one magical piece!

Some waste is dangerous because it is **flammable** or it **corrodes** certain materials, which then release harmful chemicals. Other waste is toxic. There are other types of hazardous waste, such as atomic waste used in power plants. This waste cannot be seen but can harm humans and wildlife. Each hazardous waste type requires different treatments for effective recycling.

HERO OR VILLAIN?

Recycling hazardous waste seems to depend on where you live. For example, California considers cell phones to be hazardous, but other states do not. Some nations classify tires as hazardous, but others don't. And no one seems to classify plastics as hazardous! So, it is clear that a lot of harmful waste still ends up in a dump, in a landfill site, or as billowing toxic smoke and fumes.

⌄ Old refrigerators that corrode or are broken up release chlorofluorocarbon (CFC) gases that rise into the atmosphere, destroying a layer of gas called ozone. The ozone layer filters out harmful rays from the Sun that burn living things on Earth.

How is hazardous waste recycled?

Some hazardous waste, such as zinc, is recycled without being processed. As zinc is **smelted**, zinc dust rises from the furnace through special chimneys that return it for re-smelting. Paint waste, on the other hand, needs to be processed. Paint waste of the same color can be mixed with additives at high speed. It is then filtered and repackaged for sale. Used motor oils are filtered to remove any dirt and then processed to remove chemicals and water. Then they are refined into usable motor oil. Household batteries contain many different useful parts, such as metals and plastics. These are separated out and recycled. Even plutonium and uranium waste from atomic power stations can be captured and reused to create more energy.

⌄ Barrels of toxic waste are waiting to be analyzed and processed. This waste should not end up in landfill sites, but sometimes it does.

Did you know?

In 2011, the United States recycled 1.5 million tons of hazardous waste. That still leaves a lot of the country's hazardous waste untreated. One in six Americans lives within 1 mile (1.5 kilometers) of a toxic waste site.

But is recycling hazardous waste effective when it involves complex processes and energy and still leaves a lot of hazardous waste behind? This leftover waste has to be burned in incinerators, locked up in blocks of cement, or put into toxic waste dumps. As we have seen, a lot of it ends up in poorer countries. But richer countries cannot escape the problems of toxic waste dumps totally (see the "Did you know?" box).

BIOGRAPHY

Philip Clapp (1953–2008)
Philip Clapp was a passionate environmentalist. He was very concerned about toxic waste and its effect on the planet. For 10 years, he ran the U.S. Energy and Environment Task Force and for 14 years, the National Environmental Trust.

⌄ Used car tires can be ground into granules and added to road surfaces. They make the roads quieter to drive on.

What happens to our cell phones and computers?

What happens when we no longer want our computers, video game consoles, cell phones, or TVs? These products all have something in common—they are powered by electricity. When we throw them away, they become "e-waste."

It is important to recycle e-waste since the world now produces so much, and most e-waste goods contain parts that can be recycled. Cell phones, for example, contain valuable metals that can be extracted and melted down. Electronic components from circuit boards can be reclaimed and reused.

Eyewitness

"In China's Shantou City, 24 charcoal stoves line three walls of a workshop. On the fourth wall, five tons of circuit boards are piled high, waiting to be processed. The boards are 'roasting' over searing-hot coal fires. The workers are bent over them with soldering irons, teasing out the components, surrounded by acidic smells from soaring smoke."
From a study by scientists from China and the United States, 2010

But recycling e-waste is a huge problem because it can be dangerous work, especially when recovering components from circuit boards. These boards are "roasted" at very high temperatures and release toxins, some of which can cause lung diseases and cancers.

Did you know?

The United Nations Step Initiative reported that, in 2013, nearly 55 million tons of e-waste was created across the globe. That's about 15 pounds (7 kilograms) for every person on the planet.

Japan and some European countries have passed "take back" laws that force manufacturers to recycle their products. In the United States, some computer manufacturers have set up the Silicon Valley Toxics Coalition to recycle their products responsibly. Hewlett Packard even has its own recycling depots in California and Tennessee.

⋙ A lot of e-waste is sent illegally from rich countries to poorer ones for recycling.

How Effective Is Water Recycling?

What happens when we turn on a faucet or pull out a sink plug? Do we think about the wasted water that drains away? Can it be recycled? Happily, we can recycle this "**gray water**." We can even recycle sewage, or "black water," too. And when 1 in 8 people worldwide do not have access to safe, clean drinking water, water recycling is a top priority.

Wealthy countries install huge wastewater treatment plants in rural areas, but in the United States alone, these consume 3 to 4 percent of the nation's energy. So, smaller systems have been designed. Some people install gray-water recycling systems in their homes.

One of the most effective of these systems drains the wastewater into an underground **septic tank**, which has three compartments. The first compartment removes grease and sludge, before the water is filtered through the other two. Finally, a sandfilter purifies it further so that it can be used again, although it is not usually drinkable.

⌃ 1 Bligh Street in Sydney, Australia, is an office building with its own black-water recycling system.

Reed beds make great natural water purification systems. The reeds, which are a type of wetland grass, gradually absorb and process impurities from gray water piped from homes and businesses.

Modern technology now enables black-water treatment. You can see an example in the high-rise office building in the picture on page 20. Pipes take sewage from the building and also from the underground sewage system in the street below. It is then pumped through membranes and **ultraviolet (UV) light** treatment to clean it. The recycled water is returned to the building to flush toilets and as part of its cooling system. We need much more of this type of technology to make water recycling more effective.

HERO OR VILLAIN?

Do we need to use expensive recycling equipment? Some experts say that this equipment uses a lot of unnecessary energy. It could be more effective to use simple pipes that divert gray water from bathroom sinks and showers to flush toilets and water the yard. Rainwater can be harvested simply, too, along gutters and drainage pipes connected to barrels.

Is It Effective to Recycle Building Materials?

Are there any empty buildings where you live? Do you wonder what might happen to the waste if they are demolished? There is a huge amount of building waste all over the world. But is it effective to reclaim and recycle it?

Buildings offer a wide range of recyclable materials, including brick, stone, concrete, wood, metals, and glass. All these can be broken down, smelted, or melted. Recycling them saves people from **quarrying** and mining new, nonrenewable materials such as clay, stone, and lime. Metals used in construction, such as lead and copper, are valuable and reclaimable. Iron, too, is worth recovering.

⌄ Old bricks, tiles, stone, and wooden beams can be cleaned up and reused.

You might think that towns and cities would see the value of recycling building materials, but few make it compulsory. However, there are some forward-thinking places, such as the city of San Francisco, California. Here, construction and demolition recycling was made compulsory through laws passed in 2006.

Did you know?

According to the United Nations Environment Programme (UNEP), the building industry uses 3.3 billion tons of raw materials every year. It takes up 20 percent of global water usage and is responsible for 30 percent of harmful gas emissions.

Unfortunately, recycling some materials, such as concrete and brick, produces dust that is harmful to health. Other materials, like the insulating material asbestos, are so harmful they cannot be recycled at all, but they still need to be removed. Should we be concentrating as much on developing safer materials as we do on recycling?

⟩ Concrete can be crushed and used for **aggregate**, which is laid down as a building material for roads and the foundations of buildings.

⌃ The main supports and frame for this home in Uruguay use guadua bamboo, which is a sustainable, biodegradable, and strong building material.

Why don't we use more recycled building materials?

Why do most wealthy countries rely so much on building with new materials? It is partly because there is little training in building techniques that use recycled materials. Thankfully, things are slowly changing. Illinois Central College, in East Peoria, Illinois, is launching a certificate program in Deconstruction and Building Materials Salvage and Reuse. This new field of study was put in place following the destruction of over 1,000 homes during a vicious tornado that ripped through the town of Washington, Illinois.

> "It's atrocious what's happening in Washington. Driving through and seeing the debris—so many materials are there. We need to ensure...that these materials don't need to go to the landfill."
>
> Anne Nicklin, instructor, Illinois Central College, East Peoria

Did you know?

At the site of the London 2012 Olympics, 98.5 percent of demolition waste was recycled before building began. The building foundations for the Olympic Stadium, Aquatics Center, and Handball Arena used 30 percent recycled concrete.

Unfortunately, most recycled materials still need to be mixed or joined together with new nonrenewable materials. So, shouldn't we be investing more money in growing or developing more **sustainable** building materials? Already, in many countries, sustainable forests are providing wood. New saplings are being planted to replace the trees that have been used in construction. There are also some new, exciting developments. In South and Central America, the massive, fast-growing guadua bamboo plant is becoming a fashionable, sustainable material. Architects are designing more buildings especially for this strong, water-resistant plant.

>> More than 80 percent of soil on London's Olympic Park site was cleaned and reused.

How Effective Is Food Recycling?

What can you do with food that is old and no longer edible? And what about the food left on your plate? You might be surprised to know that it can all be recycled! This type of waste is known as **biowaste**, or biodegradable waste, and is now collected and recycled in many countries. But is it effective?

Did you know?

You can make your own compost heap in your yard or on a balcony. The instructions are on a web site listed on page 46. Ask an adult to help you.

⌃ On the East African coast, coconuts provide food and juice. The fibers around the husks, and the leaves on the palms, are made into ropes and mats. Nothing is wasted.

First, we need to ask ourselves why we waste so much food? The food on your plate is the result of a journey from fields to your home. At each stage, there is wastage. In developing countries, over 40 percent of food never reaches the plate because it is lost after harvesting and during processing. In richer countries, more than 40 percent is wasted during retail and consumption.

Fortunately, food can be very effectively recycled because it is made of living plants or animals, which makes it easily biodegradable. This means it can be broken down naturally by **bacteria** and other **microorganisms**. Uncooked fruits and vegetables are best separated from cooked foods because they biodegrade more quickly into compost, which helps plants to grow. As both cooked and uncooked food break down, they release gases, especially methane, that can be used for fuel.

Did you know?

At Purdue University in West Lafayette, Indiana, scientists are rolling out an amazing, portable energy-making machine. It uses three technologies to produce energy from waste. It turns food into ethanol, a biofuel. It makes methane and propane gas from paper and plastics, and it has a diesel engine that burns gas, ethanol, and diesel fuel. Its engine powers a generator that produces electricity on-site. Amazing!

Is bioenergy the best end-product for recycled food?

Bioenergy uses processed plant matter to produce fuels called biofuels. Many scientists and environmentalists believe that producing biofuels is good for the planet. This is because plants absorb carbon gases from the atmosphere as they grow. After recycling, carbon gases are then released from these same plants when they are used as fuels. This is called being **carbon neutral**. But is this the whole story? Carbon emissions are also produced when transporting and processing the biowaste, so it is hard to know for sure how the figures stack up.

Nevertheless, recycling food has produced some exciting results. On a local level, people are setting up small recycling machines for filtering and refining used cooking oil, which can power vehicles. In cities, biogas refineries are providing much-needed cheap energy. In the Norwegian city of Oslo, experts have figured out that 2.2 pounds (1 kilogram) of food waste produce over half a gallon (0.5 liter) of biofuel, which they use to fuel their buses.

⌄ If the city of Oslo, Norway, recycles all its stored waste, it will be able to power 135 buses for a year.

Are we doing enough to stop food from being wasted?

Over 30 percent of all food produced worldwide each year gets lost or wasted. That's about 1.4 billion tons. Every year, consumers in rich countries waste 245 million tons of food.

In 2011, in the United States alone, only 4 percent of the total 36 million tons of food waste was composted. The rest ended up in landfill sites or burned in incinerators. In landfill sites, this waste emits 20 percent of the country's methane gas as it rots. And methane is 21 times more harmful to our climate than carbon dioxide.

> **It is outrageous that [almost 100 million tons] of perfectly fine food gets wasted each year, while an estimated 79 million people in the EU [European Union] live beneath the poverty line and around 16 million depend on food aid from charitable institutions.**
> Liam Aylward, from the Fianna Fáil Party, Ireland

Across the Atlantic, in the 28 countries that make up the European Union, 98 million tons of food are wasted every year.

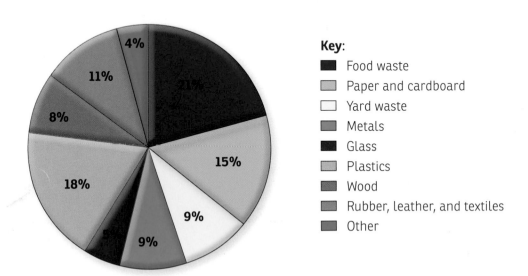

Key:
- ■ Food waste
- ▨ Paper and cardboard
- □ Yard waste
- ▨ Metals
- ■ Glass
- ▨ Plastics
- ▨ Wood
- ▨ Rubber, leather, and textiles
- ▨ Other

≫ You can see from this pie chart that in 2012, 21 percent of all landfill in the United States was food waste.

HERO OR VILLAIN?

Farmers in rich nations produce a lot of food. Yet in these countries, millions of people cannot afford to buy enough to eat. Perhaps we should concentrate on making sure everyone has enough money to buy food rather than recycling food waste. In the developing world, farmers could be helped to modernize food harvesting, storing, and processing. This way, less food would be lost.

⌄ Food waste can be a health hazard. It can attract rats and insects and cause disease.

Do We Recycle Packaging Effectively?

Are you amazed at the amount of packaging that comes with the things you buy? Packaging forms much of the world's most damaging waste. In terms of plastics alone, over 30 percent of all plastics are produced for packaging! How can we all be encouraged to recycle more? And is it worth it?

Maybe what we need is a good example to encourage us. In 2011, Belgium managed to recycle an amazing 80.2 percent of all its packaging. So, how do they do it?

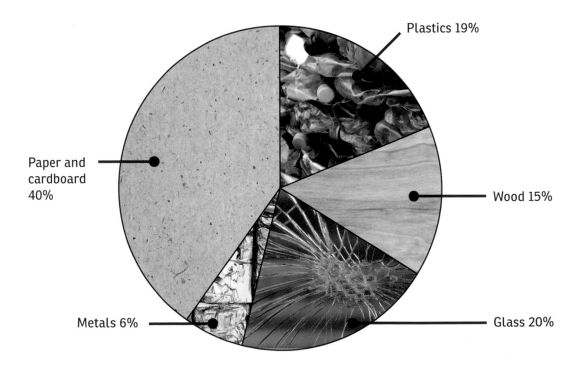

Plastics 19%

Wood 15%

Glass 20%

Metals 6%

Paper and cardboard 40%

⌃ You can see that in the European Union, paper and cardboard packaging waste are twice the volume of any other type. But they are not too difficult to recycle.

One of the keys to their success was making industries responsible for their packaging waste. So, Belgian companies got together and set up Fost Plus. This organization cooperates with local governments, private waste management companies, and recyclers to collect and recycle all household packaging. It includes glass, paper, cardboard, plastic bottles and flasks, aluminum and steel packaging, and drink cartons. Paper, cardboard, and glass are taken straight to recycling companies, and the rest goes to specialized recyclers.

BIOGRAPHY

William Booth (1829–1912)
In 1865, William Booth founded the Salvation Army, a Christian organization set up to help poor people in London. Booth started up the Household Salvage Brigade, collecting and reselling unwanted household goods to help finance his charity work. The Salvation Army sells recycled goods to this day.

Can recycling all packaging be effective—and in all places?

Some types of packaging, such as cardboard and glass, are far easier to recycle than others. It takes less energy to recycle some materials than it does to make identical new ones. But this doesn't necessarily mean that all recycling of packaging is effective.

The United Kingdom, for example, recovers and recycles a lot of green glass from imported wine bottles. But the United Kingdom itself only has a small wine industry that does not need that many recycled bottles. Some of the bottles are **down-cycled** into sand used for filters and aggregate for the construction industry. The United Kingdom now also imports more wine in huge containers and then bottles it using recycled glass. But it still has a lot of green glass!

⋁ Cardboard and paper can be shredded and reprocessed into more packaging, or compacted into insulation for homes.

Packaging can be important for hygiene, protection, safety, and keeping a product fresh for a long time. It is also a very effective way to promote a product. There are other issues, too. Let's go back to polystyrene. Keeping a ceramic cup clean uses far more energy and carbon emissions than a polystyrene one, whether it is recycled or not!

We saw on page 12 that polystyrene foam used to make cups is really difficult to recycle. It's also a problem to transport. The foam is bulky, so it takes up a lot of space in a recovery truck, and therefore it often costs too much to take it to any faraway recycling depot. This is unfortunate, because after compression, recycled polystyrene can be processed into usable plastic pellets for insulation sheets in buildings.

Are There Effective Alternatives to Recycling?

Recycling saves a lot of the world's precious nonrenewable resources. With some materials, it costs less time and energy to recycle than to make new. But with others, recycling is not so effective. So, are there better alternatives?

Let's take a step back. Before we need to recycle, why don't we just reduce the amount of products we buy? Why don't we reuse things more—perhaps in a different way? This is known as repurposing. Or why don't we just refuse to accept or buy the products that are most harmful to our planet, such as plastic bags?

>> In South Africa, people make jewelry, stylish bags, and other craft pieces, like this chicken, out of plastic bags.

⌃ Making jute bags in Bangladesh provides much-needed employment.

In Bangladesh, the government has taken a stand and banned plastic bags completely. Instead, it is promoting bags made out of **jute**, which is a natural plant fiber crop grown locally. In Ireland, consumers have to pay 15 Eurocents (about 20 cents) per plastic bag. This has been incredibly effective and reduced usage by 90 percent in the first year!

Plastic bag waste can be reduced in easy ways. Others take a bit more thought, such as fashionable "upcycling." This means making something special from old, unwanted items or materials. Kenya has been at the forefront of upcycling since it produced a desirable range of sandals made from disused car tires. Upcycling uses few processes and has little cost to the environment. Repurposing and upcycling is the norm in most developing countries.

> " Recycling? I call it down-cycling. They smash bricks, they smash everything. What we need is upcycling, where old products are given more value, not less. "
>
> Reiner Pilz, German engineer and upcycler, who first used the term "upcycling" in 1994

How can we make recycling more effective?

Even when we do reduce, reuse, or refuse products, there is still a lot of waste. How can this be recycled more effectively? One way is to simplify waste sorting. In our homes, it is easier if we don't have to sort trash into a lot of different containers for recycling. In the 1990s, cities in California began experimenting with "single stream recycling." This means that people can mix all their recycling into one bin, apart from food and yard waste. It has been extremely effective.

Did you know?

Modern sorting technology is making recycling much more effective. This waste sorter uses sensors to identify waste materials and uses jets of air to push each type into the correct container.

One of the most successful cities is San Francisco, which now recycles or creates energy using 80 percent of its waste and aims to have zero waste by 2020. The city's 200,000-square-foot (18,580-square-meter) recycling plant processes an average of 750 tons of paper, plastic, glass, and metals a day!

There are some successful examples of waste collection in industry, too. In 2005, Walmart, the world's largest retail company, experimented with a "sandwich bale" of waste between large pieces of cardboard. This made the waste easier to collect from stores and to deposit at recycling depots. Walmart now recycles a huge percentage of its waste.

A mechanized conveyor belt has improved recycling figures and working conditions for pickers at this landfill site in Brazil.

What's the Verdict on Recycling?

So, do we really know if recycling is effective all over the world? It's hard for developing countries to spend money on waste statistics, but wealthier countries are able to provide data showing the need for serious changes.

For example, in the United States, a recent study shows that the way we produce, deliver, obtain, and dispose of goods leads to 42 percent of greenhouse gas emissions. But how can we change this pattern for the better? Reducing waste is important. Designing products and packaging that are easier to recycle will also help.

> **If it can't be reduced, reused, repaired, rebuilt, refurbished, refinished, resold, recycled, or composted, then it should be restricted, redesigned, or removed from production.**
>
> Pete Seeger (1919–2014), American singer, songwriter, and environmentalist

BIOGRAPHY

Zhang Yin (born 1957)
Zhang Yin was born in China, where she set up Nine Dragons Paper Holdings Limited. This recycling company makes boxes from waste paper shipped in from the United States. These boxes are filled with goods and then exported! Zhang is one of the most successful businesswomen in the world.

Do you think we need more laws and a firmer approach? We have seen that San Francisco has very effective recycling—but it is also very tough! Since 2009, the city made recycling compulsory for all residents, businesses, and industries. If this could be spread across the world, maybe recycling would be much more effective. What do you think?

⌃ It's Earth Day, and everyone's helping to pick up waste!

Quiz

How much do you remember about recycling from reading this book? You could find out by answering these questions. You can use the index to help you. Some of the answers might lie in the boxes and captions as well as the main text.

1 Which of these substances does not break down easily?

   A cardboard
   B plastic
   C fruit
   D wood

2 How can we best use composted food waste?

   A We can use it to insulate buildings.
   B We can mix it with soil to help plants grow.
   C We can leave it in landfill sites to rot down more.
   D We can dump it into the sea.

3 Which gas emitted from landfill sites harms our atmosphere and contributes to climate change most?

   A methane
   B nitrogen oxide
   C oxygen
   D sulfur dioxide

4 Which of these plastic items can be recycled easily?

   A a hot-drink cup made of plastic foam
   B a waterproof jacket made of nylon
   C a bottle made of a plastic polymer
   D a toothbrush holder made of acrylic

5 What harm do chlorofluorocarbon (CFC) gases found in refrigerators do?

   A CFC gases create ground level fog that has dangerous toxins in it.
   B CFC gases cause breathing problems in humans.
   C CFC gases cause toxic rain-bearing clouds to form.
   D CFC gases reduce ozone levels in the atmosphere, letting in harmful rays from the Sun.

6 Which type of plant can purify wastewater?

- **A** reed
- **B** wheat
- **C** eucalyptus
- **D** rye grass

7 Which building material is so harmful that it cannot be recycled?

- **A** cement
- **B** lead
- **C** copper
- **D** asbestos

8 Which type of packaging uses 95 percent less energy when it is recycled than when it is made from new materials?

- **A** paper
- **B** aluminum
- **C** soft plastics
- **D** cardboard

9 Which material is being used in Bangladesh to replace plastic in bag making?

- **A** cotton
- **B** jute
- **C** corn stalks
- **D** paper

10 What does "single stream recycling" mean?

- **A** It means recycling cooked and uncooked food separately.
- **B** It means mixing all recycling into one bin and leaving it for workers on landfill sites to separate.
- **C** It means picking out just plastics for recycling.
- **D** It means mixing recycling into one bin, apart from food and yard waste.

Glossary

aggregate broken-down concrete, often reused in foundations for new buildings and as a building material for roads

bacteria tiny microorganisms that can break down materials, especially those that were once living, such as plants

biodegradable material, mostly plant and animal, that can be broken down easily

biowaste waste from plants or animals

carbon neutral substances and goods made, or processes, that balance the amount of harmful carbon gases they use with the ones they save

composted broken down plant or animal matter

corrode rust or crumble

down-cycle reuse waste to make poor-quality products

emit throw out or discharge

flammable material that easily catches fire

gray water wastewater, such as from bathroom and kitchen sinks

groundwater underground water sources

hazardous extremely harmful

jute plant crop, the fibers of which are used to make sustainable material

landfill site land used to bury waste

microorganism tiny living thing, such as bacteria, that you can only see with a microscope

pesticide chemical that destroys unwanted plants such as weeds

polymer very large molecule made up of smaller units called monomers. Plastics molecules are examples of polymers.

quarrying digging into the earth to extract materials such as stone, clay, and lime

septic tank tank that holds waste and wastewater from bathrooms and kitchens

sewage waste from bathrooms that needs to be treated before it can be reused

smelted when metal ore is extracted from the rock in which it is held. It usually involves melting at high temperatures.

solvent liquid that can dissolve something—for example, paint thinner or nail polish remover

sustainable easily or naturally renewed or reused without harm to people or the planet

toxic poisonous

ultraviolet (UV) light waves of light emitted by the Sun. Skin and plants can burn if they are exposed to ultraviolet (UV) waves, or rays, for too long.

Find Out More

If you want to find out more about recycling, take a look at some of these books and web sites. In addition to this, you could take part in any school activity or club that helps clean up your environment and reuses any waste you collect. You could also see if you can reduce the waste in your home.

Books

Gogerly, Liz. *A Teen Guide to Eco-Fashion* (Eco Guides). Chicago: Heinemann Library, 2013.

Hunter, Rebecca. *Waste and Recycling* (Eco Alert). Mankato, Minn.: Sea-to-Sea, 2012.

Rothschild, David de. *Earth Matters*. New York: Dorling Kindersley, 2011.

Websites

FactHound offers a safe, fun way to find Internet sites related to this book. All of the sites on FactHound have been researched by our staff.

Here's all you do:

Visit www.facthound.com

Type in this code: 9781484609965

Places to Visit

Local and national science and technology museums often feature exhibitions on the atmosphere, the environment, and climate change. For example, you can check out the following:

The Exploratorium, San Francisco, California
www.exploratorium.edu
The Exploratorium is a science museum with hands-on exhibits that encourage visitors to directly engage with science and issues affecting the environment.

Museum of Science, Boston, Massachusetts
www.mos.org
The Museum of Science, Boston, features many exhibits that explore issues relating to the environment and problems affecting Earth. "Conserve @ Home" shows you how you might be wasting energy in your home. "Energized!" explores natural energy sources such as the Sun, water, and wind.

The Museum of Science and Industry, Chicago, Illinois
www.msichicago.org
Here, you can explore the "Future Energy Chicago" exhibition. This begins with an explanation of different forms of energy and then allows visitors to compete to find the most environmentally friendly solutions to problems such as transportation, car design, and home design. "Earth Revealed" investigates different issues affecting our planet. The museum also features many revolving exhibits about climate and the environment.

Index